Totnes Castle

By Morten Williams

Dedicated to the late King Harold Godwinson

# Table of Contents

**Totnes Castle**

Totnes Castle stands on a 57.41 feet high manmade motte, which looms over the historic medieval town of Totnes. From its battlements, it commands a splendid and picturesque view across the town below as well as offering scenic views of wild and rugged Dartmoor. Totnes Castle is steeped in a rich and varied history and is one of the best surviving examples of a Norman motte and bailey castle. Both 'motte' and 'bailey' are old-French words, 'motte' meaning 'hill' or 'mound' while 'bailey' means 'low yard'. Due to the town's strategic position and close proximity to the River Dart, Totnes was a logical place to build a castle.

Totnes was a well-known port town and had a reputation of being one the best places to harbour a boat; this was due to how far a ship could navigate inland. Evidence of this can be found in a book called 'Historia Regum Britanniae' which was written in 1136 by Geoffrey of Monmouth. With a port, Totnes became a fairly wealthy town, as a result of this influx of prosperity, King Edward the Elder in 907 had the town fortified, this resulted in Totnes becoming one of the only fortified towns in the South West, which is evidence that Totnes started to become distinctly affluent. However later on in the town's history, the mint in Totnes at the time of 1036 (thirty years before the Norman Conquest) had ceased minting, which was an indication that the importance of the town had started to dwindle. Totnes was accorded with a royal charter by King John in 1206, which transformed Totnes into a free town. This meant that Totnes was allowed to formulate its own laws. Due to the Normans, Totnes grew to be once again a very prosperous town and in 1523 it was the second richest town in Devon and sixteenth richest town in the whole of England.

Historical photograph of Totnes Castle from the air

Judhellus, Son of Alured, who later became Judhael de Totnes, was a Breton (as opposed to a true Norman) leader of the Norman campaign in the West and was a supporter of William the Conqueror. Judhael was granted a hundred mansions in Devonshire and rule over the town of Totnes. However it does not appear that Judhael actively took part in the Battle of Hastings or the Siege of Exeter. Despite Judhael's lack of prowess in battle, in 1068 William the Conqueror gave Judhael the right to build a motte and bailey castle in Totnes. The castle was built as a direct result of the Siege of Exeter which took place in 1068, where William I marched an army of Normans and Saxons (who were loyal to William I) to the Anglo-Saxon resistance stronghold of Exeter in Devon, where Harold Godwinson's mother (Gytha Thorkelsdóttir) was held-up.

The siege ended with Gytha fleeing the country (it is possible that Gytha went back to Scandinavia) and the stronghold of Exeter agreeing to a conditional surrender. Judhael also founded Totnes Priory, the foundation charter for Totnes Priory is dated 1087, the records of this are held at the Devon Heritage Centre in Exeter. However due to the Dissolution of the Monasteries, Totnes Priory no longer stands. After the death of King William I in 1087, Judhael fell out of favour with King William II which lost him the barony of Totnes, however later on in history, roughly in 1100 Judhael was granted the feudal barony of Barnstaple, this was once again a barony position in Devon. Judhael then founded the priory in Barnstaple 1107. Judhael was married to Bertha de Totnes; they had a daughter, Eleanor de Totnes, who may also have been known as Eleanor de Barnstaple.

Totnes Castle was originally of wooden construction, which saw the inner bailey surrounded by a wooden palisade as a defensive measurement. A wooden draw-bridge connected the inner bailey to the outer bailey. Between the inner and outer bailey a moat was dug with very steep banks, which can still be seen today. The depth of the moat is unknown. A second smaller moat surrounded the base of the motte; however this has since been filled in. The keep at the top of the motte was home to a wooden square shaped watchtower, which stood on a stone foundation (which is still visible). The tower construction was simple yet effective, on top of the dry-stone foundations (which go down into the motte by approximately 11ft; however the foundations may go down to the base of the motte), large wooden sleeper beams were placed, on top of which then sat the wooden watchtower. The height of the watchtower is unknown but it would have been higher than the crenellations. The tower could have possibly had a room built into it for storage of equipment and for sleeping in and the outside of the tower may have had a daub rendering. All the buildings such as stables, smithy, the grand hall and barracks were in the inner bailey. No one lived in the keep itself. Remarkably, the whole site only took a month to be constructed. The Bayeux Tapestry depicts motte and bailey castles very clearly, scene 45 depicts a motte and bailey castle being constricted, this scene is particularly good as it gives some indication of the tools and methods used. The caption for scene 45 reads 'Iste jussit ut foderetur castellum at hestenga' which translates roughly as 'He ordered that a motte should be dug at Hastings.'

In the 13th century roughly in 1219 Totnes Castle saw much rebuilding and refortification. During this period the timber keep and timber palisade were replaced with stone counterparts, however it was reported that the stone shell keep was of a weak construction. The wooden watchtower was also dismantled. In 1250 the castle fell into ruin due to being neglected. A rudimentary lean-to shelter had collapsed inside the keep and some of the outer walls of the bailey had also fallen into disrepair.

During the 14th century roughly in 1326 by order of King Edward II of England, the site was once again completely rebuilt and refortifications were made, however this time the changes to the structures were far more robust than the alterations done in the early 13th century. The stone keep is roughly 70ft in internal diameter and was built on the site of the timber keep. From 1326, the keep has stood firm ever since. The outside of the stone keep may have been whitewashed. Surprisingly the curtain wall which runs up the side of the motte and ends at the entrance to the keep is also in a good state of repair. Throughout its history, the castle never saw action. The stone keep is constructed out of limestone rubble and red sandstone. The stone for its construction was possibly sourced from Dartmoor and the Torbay area of Devon.

The order of refortification by King Edward II in 1326 stated 'Quod castrum uestrum de Toteneys hominibus as arma, uictualibus, armaturis et omnibus aliis necessariis, muniri et foriticari faciatis'. Which roughly translated into English states 'Your castle of Totnes, which men, arms, supplies and all that is necessary, make fortifications and make strong'. During 1326, the wife of King Edward II, Isabella of France (also known as the She-Wolf of France) who allied herself with Roger Mortimer, 1st Earl of March, led a campaign against King Edward II. This was known as the Despenser War, in which the reign of King Edward II crumbled and in 1327, the king abdicated his crown.

However, using all available sources, it is not impossible to theorise that the stone keep which was constructed in the 13th century, could have been of a very good constriction. King Edward II uses the phrase 'make fortifications and make strong' which can suggest that only further fortifications were added rather than starting a brand new keep. The keep has 6ft thick walls, which in the 13th century would have provided adequate defence against siege weapons of that period. However it would have offered little to no defence against 14th century siege weapons, which is another indication that the current keep is in fact, 13th century.

Historical photograph of the keep's interior. The wooden railings have been removed and since been replaced by metal safety railings

Inside the stone keep there is the garderobe, which was small space to store valuable items and equipment. It also functioned as a place to sleep as well as to be used as a toilet. There is an arrow-loop built into the garderobe wall, this was a narrow opening to admit light, it also functioned as a slit to release arrows through. The word 'garderobe' derives from the French word for 'wardrobe'. There are two staircases leading up to the battlements, these are located either side of the one and only entrance into the keep. Jutting out along the wall, almost flush to the battlement walkway are a few stones, these stones are called corbels and would have been supporting an oak beamed and slated roof for a lean-to shelter, this shelter was built in the northwest area of the keep, close to the garderobe. There are 33 crenels, 34 merlons and 22 arrow slits which make the crenulations of the keep's battlements. The crenels are the indentations and the merlons are the raised sections. The term 'cranny' comes from the word crenel which means 'notch'.

Totnes Castle would have been defended with ranged weaponry, mostly bows and crossbows, which is why the merlons at Totnes Castle are shielded to offer maximum protection to the archers up on the battlements. Square openings, called embrasures, can be found in different locations in the keep's wall, garderobe and stairways. Embrasures are openings for line of sight, admitting light and they could also be possibly used by archers to release arrows through. The 72 stone steps leading up to the shell keep are a relatively new addition to the motte, before the introduction of the stone steps (possibly introduced by the Victorians as it seems unlikely they were installed by the Ministry of Works) there would have been a steep wooden walkway which ran up (parallel to the curtain wall) to the keep. There are 16 steps leading up to the battlements within the keep.

The Ministry of Works in 1954 commissioned an excavation of the site by Mr S.E Rigold. Inside the keep, a few stake-holes were excavated close to the remains of a hearth; these holes were up to 8 inches deep and roughly 1 inch in diameter. Some of these holes, it has been suggested, were remains of a wattle screen which would have screened something from the hearth. More holes suggested that there may have been, possibly, a loom, yet no loom weights were found to back up this theory. Yet, it is not impossible to conceive the notion that the wattle screen was erected to shield a loom. However the excavation unearthed a spindle-whorl from the same area, which shows that people may have been present up in the keep and spinning wool.

A spindle-whorl is a small weight designed to weight a spindle. They are spherical in shape and designed to maintain a consent spin or to increase the spin. Spindle-whorls can be made of many materials such as bone or even glass. The material used to manufacture the Spindle-whorls was not documented; however they could have been made from of limestone or red sandstone.

A smaller site survey was carried out in February 1999; this survey was not as detailed as the Excavation carried out by Mr S.E Rigold. The motte suffered from a landslide on the 16th January 1999, which if not dealt with in a timely manner, could have resulted in a total destabilisation and collapse of the motte. While the restoration work was carried out, it presented an excellent opportunity to discover more about the motte. A great deal more information was discovered about the motte's construction which further helped piece together the site's history. A number of coins and late Saxon and early Norman pottery were found during the survey. Late Saxon and early Norman refuse was unearthed as well, in the form of charcoal and animal bones.

The Ministry of Works Excavation by Mr S.E Rigold - 1954

Over time the castle once again stopped being used and by the end of the medieval period it slipped into a state of disrepair and neglect. The dwellings and other buildings, such the stables, hall and barracks for the soldiers were reported to be in ruins. However the stone keep and most of the curtain wall still remained in serviceable condition. In 1642 to 1646 the keep once again saw use during the English Civil War. It was occupied by the Royalist 'cavalier' troops, however in 1645 it was gutted by parliamentary army 'New model Army' led by Sir Thomas Fairfax, 3rd Lord Fairfax of Cameron. Sir Thomas Fairfax was the general and parliamentary commander-in-chief. In 1646 the Guild Hall in Totnes was used by Sir Thomas Fairfax (whose nickname was 'Black Tom') and Oliver Cromwell (whose nickname was 'Old Ironsides' and from 1653 was the Lord Protector of the Commonwealth of England, Scotland, and Ireland) for strategic deliberations. Inside the Guild Hall there are wooden tables made of oak, which were used by Sir Thomas Fairfax and Oliver Cromwell. The Guild Hall was constructed in 1553 on the ruins of the medieval priory, which Judhael de Totnes founded.

After the English Civil War, the castle once again ceased to be used. In 1764 Edward Seymour, 9th Duke of Somerset purchased the castle and the nearby property Berry Pomeroy, the castle and Berry Pomeroy at this point were both in a state of disrepair. During the 1920s a section of ground was levelled in the inner bailey for a tennis court, there was also a tea room. During the 1940s, the grounds were used to home evacuees. During this period of time, Italian prisoners of war were set the task of maintaining the site. The Italian prisoners of war carved names and dates into a tree in the inner bailey, which you can still see today. Although the tree is now dead from an infection and lost most of its bark, so only a few of the engravings remain. Then in 1947, Percy Hamilton Seymour, 18th Duke of Somerset, passed Totnes Castle on to the Ministry of Works. In the end, Totnes Castle ended up in the hands of English Heritage in 1984, who still own the site.

# Flora and Fauna of Totnes Castle

The Victorians drastically altered the castle grounds over the years by turning it into a small arboretum with trees they brought back from their Grand Tours. One of the more notable trees which the Victorians brought back is the Mediterranean holly oak (Quercus ilex), which is an evergreen. This particular variety of tree was first planted in the country at Mamhead Park (a stately home) located in Dawlish in Devon. This tree once dominated the inner bailey where it stands, however now it is not in good health. Other trees in the castle grounds include a Victorian plane tree.

The castle has seen much deforestation, as during the early 20th century the motte as well as inside the keep was heavily wooded with a vast variety of trees. But sometime during the late 20th and early 21st century, a vast swaft of trees were removed. The deforestation was carried out to insure that the site remained intact as the trees on the motte and inside the keep could have over time, made the motte and keep unstable and this could have led a great deal of subsidence. English Heritage still maintains the motte, bailey and the moat; however this task is only carried out once a year by specialists. The grass within the inner bailey is regularly cut during the year, with areas left for wildlife to thrive.

Totnes Castle is home to numerous Grey Squirrels (Sciurus carolinensis), European Badgers (Meles meles) and Red Foxes (Vulpes vulpes). Due to the uncut areas on the motte, inner bailey and areas around the moat, wild flowers are free to grow. The wild flowers are home to such insects as the Cinnabar Caterpillar and moth (Tyria jacobaeae) which enjoys the patches of Ragwort which grows on the motte, Small White (Pieris rapae), Large White (Pieris brassicae) and occasionally the Red Admiral (Vanessa atalanta) can also be found in the grounds.

Attached to the many trees within the inner bailey are bat boxes as the site is home to two types of bat. They are the Common Pipistrelle (Pipistrellus pipistrellus) and the Lesser Horseshoe (Rhinolophus hipposideros).

An aerial view of a heavily forested Totnes Castle

A historic view of the keep's interior, besieged by vegetation

## Historical Photographs of Totnes Castle

**Historical photograph of the motte and keep after deforestation**

**An early photograph of the picturesque entrance to Totnes Castle**

The Castle, Totnes, by Floodlight

103

An early photograph of the keep illuminated by floodlight

Norman and Saxon reenactors at Totnes Castle - 1960s

The interior of the keep - 1998

**An Honourable Mention**

It should be mentioned that if it wasn't for the Battle of Stamford Bridge, which took place on 25th September 1066, the Norman Conquest may not have been a successful campaign for William I. King Harold Godwinson travelled up to Stamford in order to do battle with his brother (Tostig Godwinson) and King Harald Hardrada. During the battle the Norwegian invaders had been defeated and Tostig and Hardrada were killed. If this battle had not taken place, King Harold would have been in the right place at the right time to repel the Norman invaders. However three weeks after the Battle of Stamford Bridge, King Harold was defeated by the Normans at the Battle of Hastings on 14th October 1066, it was this battle which claimed the life of King Harold Godwinson.

**Resources Used**

- Mr S.E Rigold Totnes Castle Excavation Report (1954)

- Devon Heritage Centre in Exeter

- Department of Environment Totnes Castle Pamphlet by Mr S.E Rigold (1975)

- English Heritage Pamphlet by Mr S.E Rigold (1990)

- 'Historia Regum Britanniae' By Geoffrey of Monmouth (1136)

- 'William the Conqueror' by David R Bates (2004)

- Totnes image Bank Trust (Charity Number: 1082531)

- English Heritage Totnes Castle Guidebook By Stewart Brown (1999)

- 'The history of Totnes priory & medieval town, Devonshire, together with the sister priory of Tywardreath, Cornwall' by Watkin, Hugh Robert (1914)

- 'Butterflies of Europe' by Morten Williams (2018)

- Bayeux Tapestry Museum

- 'The Beauties of England and Wales' by John Britton and Edward Wedlake Brayley (1803)

- 'The Road to Crecy: The English Invasion of France, 1346' by Marilyn Livingstone and Morgen Witzel (2005)

- Research notes written after numerous visits to Totnes Castle and Totnes Guild Hall

**Index**